Cooler Than My Kids

Cooler Than My Kids

A HANDBOOK FOR HIP DADS

PAUL SYMONS

WILDFIRE

First published in 2025 by Wildfire
An imprint of Headline Publishing Group Limited

1

Hardback ISBN 9781035424078
ebook ISBN 9781035424085

Designed and set by EM&EN
Printed and bound in Great Britain by Clays Ltd, Elcograf S.p.A.

Headline's policy is to use papers that are natural, renewable and recyclable
products and made from wood grown in well-managed forests and other
controlled sources. The logging and manufacturing processes are expected
to conform to the environmental regulations of the country of origin.

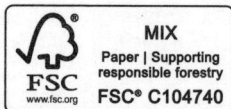

MIX
Paper | Supporting
responsible forestry
FSC
www.fsc.org
FSC® C104740

Headline Publishing Group Limited
An Hachette UK Company
Carmelite House
50 Victoria Embankment
London EC4Y 0DZ

The authorised representative in the EEA is Hachette Ireland,
8 Castlecourt Centre, Dublin 15, D15 XTP3, Ireland (email: info@hbgi.ie)

www.headline.co.uk
www.hachette.co.uk

To my wife and daughters,

who – spoiler alert – are even cooler than me

Contents

Introduction

Welcome to the age of the Ultra-Modern Dad

There was a time when a man knew what to do when he had children, settled down and left his younger years behind. It almost happened automatically. Overnight, the battered leather jacket of his youth magically transformed into a sensible anorak, his record collection turned into a set of golf clubs and he'd trade in his vintage Vespa for a reliably dull Vauxhall. Before long, he'd find himself in a cluster of fellow dads at social gatherings, animatedly discussing the best route to Cirencester while avoiding the roadworks at Swindon.

He might occasionally wonder what the hell just happened – after all, these dads extolling the joys of the A417 were once the guys he used to go raving with – but that was what fatherhood was all about, right? Experimenting and enjoying yourself was a shallow habit to be outgrown, and then replaced with less frivolous adult concerns like fixed-rate mortgages and school catchment areas. Fatherhood meant swapping cool for comfy, popular for practical and stylish for safe as the baton of edginess was passed to the next generation. It was time to be less John Lydon and more John Lewis. Everyone knew the rules.

But for a significant number of us those rules no longer apply. For the men who Get It, the onset of parenthood doesn't mean the end of being trendy and the start of turning into their own fathers. These men are not and never will be interested in their lawns, giant train sets or books about naval history. They have sworn to prolong their youthful outlook well into their parenting years, from their thirties to their fifties and beyond.

Through a series of unsubtle visual cues, these men – men like *us*, reader – rail against middle age, rage against the dying of our fashionable light, and are determined to show the world – through our footwear, bicycles and kitchen appliances – that we remain at the vanguard of what's Really Hot Right Now.

Once you start to notice us, it's not so much that we are everywhere (we might be in Islington but are less likely to be in Ipswich) as that we are a distinctive type. We are the latest and quite possibly the Last Great Men's Style Tribe.
First came the dandies, then the teddy boys, the hippies and punks. And now here we are: the Ultra-Modern Dads (UMDs) – or Hipster Dads – with our teeny-weeny beanies, vintage campervans, guitar collections and greying hair. And we have Still Got It – whatever It is.

It's not all about clothes and craft beer, looking just so and spending beyond our family's means. More than anything, the Ultra-Modern Dad is defined by an obsession with heritage and authenticity (the fact that our self-image is entirely manufactured is irrelevant). We are on a quest for The Best, especially when the best is something most people haven't heard of or wouldn't appreciate even if they had: the best music festival, the best coffee beans, the best trainers, the best dog.

We are at war with naffness, ugliness, cheapness and boringness. We are physically repulsed by anything downmarket or mass market (although we do love a flea market and a farmer's market). The stuff that everyone else likes brings us out in hives. Mainstream Dad, with his sensible car/cagoule/kids, is our nemesis. We like to think we're unique, a snowflake in selvedge denim – which we often are, until we go to see The National play live and realise there are approximately 3,000 men exactly like us in the same what3words geocode.

Although we take fatherhood extremely seriously, our relationship with the younger generation, including our own children, is complex to say the least. Don't try telling us that we're losing our edge and the kids are coming up from behind – even though those insecurities cross our mind with increasing frequency. We have a love–hate relationship with just about anyone younger than us, especially when they show signs of being almost as knowledgeable about the latest brands, bands, films, foods and fads as we are.

The Ultra-Modern Dad is a mystery inside an enigma wrapped in a Carhartt overshirt, and over the coming pages we will unlock his stylish secrets and explain what makes him tick. We'll explain what drives him and what he drives, and we will probe the UMD brain to find out what gets his pulse racing (besides midlife hypertension).

If you've Still Got It – and if you're reading this book, the chances are you have – we'll show you how to get even more of It. And if you haven't Still Got It, we'll tell you how to Get It – although if you Never Had It in the first place, Getting It at your age is going to be an uphill battle, like acquiring an eight-pack in your mid-forties or shaking off an IPA-induced hangover in under twelve hours.

We will identify the various Ultra-Modern Dad sub-groups – musical, sporty, foodie and so on. We will also explain what it's like to live with one, should your other half need reminding how lucky she is.

The checklist: tell-tale signs you're a Hipster Dad

- Your dress sense says: Oregon woodsman, Scottish Highlands boatbuilder, California semi-pro triathlete or washed-up Haçienda DJ – and possibly a combination of all four – even though most of your waking hours are spent working as an insurance broker in Penge.

- You've amassed over 200 records in your vinyl library. Not bad considering you only bought a turntable four years ago – around the same time you eBayed your old stereo and your stash of Deacon Blue and Texas CDs.

- Your dog has its own Instagram account. Your children are banned from social media.

- Your official favourite football team is based in a country you've never visited.

- Your car is remarkably similar to one that appeared in your favourite 1980s cop show. Your kids don't get the reference.

- You go to at least one gig a month, even though nowadays you need to wear earplugs and usually start craving a sit-down after twenty minutes. You always leave two songs before the end because all that toe-tapping makes your sciatica flare up.

- One of your children is named after the drummer/bassist from your favourite 1960s psych rock band.

- You occasionally 'borrow' your teenage children's clothes and secretly wish they would ask to borrow yours. (Hell will freeze over first.)

- The most popular website in your internet search history is themodernhouse.com, and is the source of regular arguments with your other half. 'Don't be ridiculous – we're not going to live in a converted gasworks on Dartmoor until Roscoe has finished his GCSEs.'

- You have a subscription to *Wallpaper**, *Fantastic Man* and *Monocle*, even though you don't really like them or understand the articles. They do amazing tote bags, though.

If it looks, sounds and acts like a midlife crisis, isn't it just a midlife crisis?

To the uneducated, the behaviour of the Ultra-Modern Dad may be indistinguishable from that of middle-aged fathers of every previous generation when faced with the harsh reality that his looks and libido are fading, his favourite musicians have started dying off and he's mathematically closer to the day of his death than the day he passed his driving test. And, in many ways, the uneducated would be right. We UMDs bear many of the symptoms of the crisis-afflicted midlife male, it's true, but that doesn't mean becoming an Ultra-Modern Dad is just a cry for help, the 21st-century equivalent of an open-neck shirt and medallion combo or having a fling with our daughter's violin teacher. And, while there are *some* similarities, there are many significant differences, as this handy chart shows.

Midlife crisis
Fancy motorbike
Ponytail
Drug problem
Sports car
Affair with young colleague
Personal trainer
Thrashing his kids at Scrabble

Fancy mountain bike
Shaved head
Craft-beer obsession
Campervan
Flirting with barista at favourite coffee shop
Parkrun
Thrashing his kids at Subbuteo

Hipster Dad
Fancy electric scooter
Heritage-brand baseball cap
Sourdough addiction
Converted NHS ambulance
Crush on Phoebe Bridgers
Saunas and ice baths
Thrashing his kids at carrom.

The Ultra-Modern Dad hall of fame:
six celebrity heroes

Everyone needs a role model or two, even those of us who are convinced we're better than 99.9 per cent of human society. And, just because we've hit middle age, we're not too old to look up to famous fathers who could teach us a thing or two about how parenthood is no barrier to being cool. Here are half a dozen of our favourite leading men.

1. **Ryan Reynolds.** It would be harsh to say that the only reason he bought a lower-league, crap-town football team was to impress his four kids, but it's notable that he keeps reminding everyone that Inez, Betty and co. are now 'obsessed with Wrexham'.

2. **Barack Obama.** Not only does he have a habit of creating regular Spotify playlists, he also feels compelled to share them with

as many people as possible to prove he's got as-good-if-not-better music taste than his daughters. Also a fan of obscure dog breeds and reckons he could be a decent film producer, given half a chance.

3. **Keith Richards.** In particular, the 1970s–80s incarnation. Has always managed to give the impression he prioritised parties over parenthood. Scores bonus points for naming his first daughter Dandelion. See also: Ultra-Modern Grandads.

4. **David Beckham.** A classic example of Ultra-Modern Dad behaviour is to encourage your offspring to pursue a cool career – chef, photographer, model, sports star, etc. – while simultaneously reminding them and the wider world that they'll never be as good at any of those things as you. Popular with the mums.

5. **Jamie Oliver.** Scores highly on the UMD scale for giving his children names most parents would only sanction for the family guinea pig: River Rocket, Buddy Bear, Petal Blossom, Daisy Boo, etc. Fancies himself a bit in the kitchen.

6. **Idris Elba.** Has the sort of cool day job his kids would be more than happy to tell their mates about, but is convinced his *real* talent is spinning the Wheels of Steel, even though most of the DJs he meets are twenty years younger. Boasts his own ironic-but-actually-not-that-ironic DJ name ('Big Dris').

Questions the Ultra-Modern Dad asks himself every single day

- Do my kids think I'm cool?
- Do my kids' friends think I'm cooler than their dads?
- Do my kids' friends' mums think I'm cooler than their husbands?
- Do the other dads think I'm cool?
- Does my wife think I'm an idiot?
- Could I build a *Grand Designs*-style eco cabin in the woods?
- How much Fred Perry is too much?
- How do I get my kids to like the taste of sriracha?
- Can I get away with buying a vintage Saab 900?
- Have I still got what it takes on the dance floor?

- Can I get away with booking a snowboarding trip to Morzine without my family?
- Should I get a Tibetan mastiff?
- Does my coffee taste any different since I started grinding my own beans?
- Should I post about being a dad on TikTok?
- Am I actually a bit naff?
- Can I convert the garage into a recording studio?
- Should I retrain as a mixologist?
- Can I convince my partner that our summer holiday should be in Greenland, not Gran Canaria?
- Do my friends think I'm having a breakdown?
- Am I actually having a breakdown?

CHAPTER ONE

Ultra-Modern Parenting

All the gear, no Ikea: becoming a Hipster Dad

As when Gregor Samsa wakes up to discover he's turned into a giant beetle, the moment a carefree young man discovers he's metamorphosed into a *parent* can throw his entire sense of identity into a terrifying existential tailspin.

He knows – from his own parents, extended family, former friends, work colleagues and all the Mainstream Dads in his orbit – what the onset of fatherhood means. And what it often means is moving from a trendy apartment to an uncool neighbourhood with bigger gardens, trading in something sporty and speedy for a sensible family runabout and finally filing his aspirations ('become famous bass player', etc.) in a box marked 'not in this lifetime'. And while becoming a father can certainly have its upsides (two whole weeks' statutory paternity leave!), navigating this

seismic shift – and accepting that he is no longer
at the centre of his own universe – can be
a traumatic experience.

But for the Ultra-Modern Dad the transition
doesn't mean becoming an entirely different
person with a whole new set of cautious, self-
denying values. Quite the opposite. The new-found
responsibility that comes with parenting solidifies
our personal commitment to all things cool.
We will double down on our hipster habits, and
every unavoidably pragmatic parenting decision
will be offset by a gleefully irresponsible act.
Selfless vs self-absorbed, safety vs danger,
practical vs impractical: everything must be in
equilibrium in accordance with Newton's Third
Law of Parental Motion.

The yin of a stairgate is counterbalanced by
the yang of a dad-sized skateboard; a musical

box with pre-programmed nursery rhymes will
be neutralised – literally – with a pair of noise-
cancelling over-ear headphones. Baby Orson
needs a milk-bottle warmer? Dad needs a beer
fridge for the office/music studio. Unlike the new
Mainstream Dad, the Ultra-Modern Dad requires
almost as much kit as his newborn progeny.

If any of the all-important baby kit required during
the first year of family life can be given a more
palatable Ultra-Modern Dad spin, it will be spun.
Sensible stroller? Not if an off-road baby buggy is
an option, ideally one that appears to have been
designed by the team behind the Tesla Cybertruck.
Emasculating unisex chest-mounted baby carrier?
Not if a camo-print baby sling is available. (The
vibe should be 'Stormzy's Banksy-designed stab-
proof Glastonbury Festival vest', not 'eunuch with
a pouch'.) Mass-produced furniture and plastic-tat
nursery decorations? Not while there's an original

mid-century Arne Jacobsen baby mobile on his eBay watchlist.

As every parent knows, having children involves the accumulation of a frightening amount of *stuff*. For the Ultra-Modern Dad, this actually isn't frightening at all. We can't get enough of stuff. Stuff is our friend, our raison d'être, our superpower. Just as long as it's *cool* stuff. In stark contrast to Mainstream Dad, us UMDs will put up fierce resistance to bland high-street chains and the sub-standard items they sell. The John Lewis baby department is our own personal torture chamber; we'd prefer to be seen skulking out of an Old Compton Street sex shop than spotted in the toys and games section of Debenhams. Ikea saps our hipster energy with such force that every bunk-bedded room-set might as well be made out of kryptonite rather than laminated chipboard.

But, for all that, don't think of the Ultra-Modern Dad as a bad parent. We are all-in when it comes to our kids' lives: there is no school event for which we won't take time off work; we'll whip out pictures of Quinn and Taffie on our phone at the slightest provocation. It goes without saying that our kids (like all kids) may grow up to despise us, but we don't want to think about that just yet.

The Ultra-Modern Dad guide to baby names

When it comes to naming our beloved offspring, Ultra-Modern Dads will spot an opportunity to unleash our unconventional creative genius and remind the wider parenting community that we're not like other fathers – though whether we will get any of our preferred names past our partner is another matter. As with so much in the UMD repertoire, we'll push the boundaries only so far, while operating within a strict set of hipster guidelines.

Two guidelines, in fact. First, we may name our child after a still-impressive cultural icon from our own youth (case in point: Liam Gallagher's son Lennon, as in John, and Damon Albarn's daughter Missy, as in Elliott).

More effective is the second approach, as pioneered by Primal Scream frontman Bobby

Gillespie. In naming his eldest son Wolf, he unwittingly created one of the primary UMD rules of child-naming: ergo, 'the Mainstream Dad dog principle'. The more it sounds like something a Mainstream Dad would name his Labrador, the more it sounds like the child of a Hipster Dad.

Satisfyingly, the rule also works in reverse, which means the more a name resembles something a blandly old-fashioned Mainstream Dad would give to his child, the more it suits an Ultra-Modern Dad's bull terrier.

UMD child name = Mainstream Dad dog name
Bandit, Buster, Coco, Vince, Rocky, Samson, Stan, Tiger, Reggie, Juno, Moose, Storm, Patch, Simba, Queenie.

Mainstream Dad child name = UMD dog name
Kevin, Katie, Neil, Harriet, Simon, Tracy, Susan, Sebastian, Debbie, Jonathan, Mary, Karen, Alan, Emma, Dave.

Frenemies at the gate: the Ultra-Modern Dad
on the school run

The microbrewery on a bleak industrial estate, the queue for the organic butchers, the second-hand vinyl fair – this is the Ultra-Modern Dad's natural habit. Somewhere we feel much more out of place is among a throng of Mainstream Dads and Mums at the school gates as we fist-bump goodbye to Finn, Frank or Florence, or wait patiently for them to emerge at the end of the day, while we shuffle uncomfortably in our Reeboks.

Most likely, we'll be the aloof-and-loving-it guy in the corner, oblivious to the Mainstream mingling going on around us, giving off 'I'm too good for you lot' energy. The only time we'll flick our sociable switch to 'on' is when we're behind the decks at the parents' charity disco (but don't ask us to play ABBA or Wham!, even in an ironic way – our only concession to nostalgia will be a nineties trip-hop megamix), or showing off our culinary skills at the school's summer fete, dishing up 'authentic' Goan fish curry using a recipe we picked up on a backpacking trip two decades earlier.

Aloofness aside, we'll be pretty easy to spot. Thick-cut specs; rugged, fold-up Micro scooter under one arm (ours, not our child's); bandana-wearing mongrel. We might be holding two moped helmets – one big, one child-sized – both looking like something Steve McQueen wore in *Le Mans*. Though, if we can get away with it and peak-hours parking restrictions allow, we'll be sitting outside the school gates in our classic 1980s Datsun/Rover, with the engine running (if the ignition was off we'd need a bump start from the other dads to restart it, and that would be mortifying).

Small faces: Ultra-Modern mini-mes

Wherever you spot an Ultra-Modern Dad, a pint-size, double-take-inducing replica won't be too far away. The UMD likes to mould his children in his own image – from the inside out.

The wider world might not be aware of the 'canon of coolness', but six-year-old Travis is (he knows it's not OK to like Ed Sheeran or Sabrina Carpenter, but that it's essential to love The Kinks, The Specials and The Jesus and Mary Chain). The little fella will have been kitted out in scaled-down, matchy-matchy versions of his dad's olive-green overshirt, white New Balances and T-shirt bearing the name of a band that broke up several years before he was born. (The committed UMD will start the mini-me programming process even earlier, with Joy Division Baby-gros and booties in the style of Joey Ramone's Converse hi-tops.)

This is not as easy as it sounds. If unsuccessful, the effect can be to make the child look like an adult with a tragic growth-hormone disorder and the dad look even older than his fast-advancing years. Or like a trendy version of Arnold Schwarzenegger and Danny DeVito in the film *Twins*. So tread carefully.

The Hipster Dad should also be aware that, sooner or later, the compulsion to create a pint-size clone may end in frustration and disappointment. As peer pressure, self-determination and puberty kick in, the Ultra-Modern Child will to a greater or lesser extent reject the canon and begin to make his/her own cultural and sartorial discoveries. Sadly, they will find it all the more pleasurable if their new interests cause their father actual physical pain.

It's an immutable rule of family life that 90 per cent of children, crippled with embarrassment, will eventually find a way to oppose everything their parents stand for, which is why, from teenage years onwards, most UMDs tend to have wilfully uncool kids, like Saffy from *Ab Fab*. There may come a time, in their late teens or early twenties, when those kids will bravely come out to their fathers and admit that they never had any interest whatsoever in New York guitar bands of the early 2000s or their old man's other most favourite things. We will tearfully bite our lip and pretend we're OK with it.

Four things Ultra-Modern Dads are likely to say to their kids on the way to/from school

1. 'Hurry up, Zowie, we need to rush home – your breakdancing tutor will be there in twenty minutes.'

2. 'Hey, Rosco, don't forget your packed lunch – it's home-made bokkeumbap with extra kimchi. Why are you pulling that face?'

3. 'Spider, what are you wearing your school tie like that for? Remember, it should be the short, thin bit that's visible, with the wide bit tucked inside your shirt. We've been through this . . .'

4. 'Stop crying, Olga. I'd have given my left arm for a backie on my dad's BMX at your age. And it's only a graze . . .'

Meet the (hipster) parent: impressing other people's kids

Why do Ultra-Modern Dads behave the way we do? In a nutshell: to impress other people – our kids, our partner (slim chance), other dads, other mums, strangers ten years younger than us. And, last but not least, our kids' friends.

The latter is easier said than done, and very much depends on the age of the friends in question. Naturally, it gets harder the older they get. Impressing our child's toddler friends is a cinch. Conjure up a couple of modelling-balloon creations ('No, it's not a frying pan – it's a Fender Stratocaster') or master an entry-level magic trick and you'll have the attendees of five-year-old Carmy's birthday party eating out of the palm of your hand. Give a group of seven-year-olds a lengthy demonstration of your DJ skills and they'll barely notice the embarrassing gulf in talent between you and Skrillex.

Beyond the age of ten it gets much more difficult. Almost overnight the tone shifts from 'Your dad is really fun!' to 'Look at your dad – he's such a dork.' But while the Mainstream Dad will accept and embrace his dorkiness, the Ultra-Modern Dad will up his game and try ever harder to impress.

This will reach its peak when our children start dating (obviously they would never use a lame word like 'dating') and bring home boyfriends and girlfriends (they never call them that either). At that point, we'll be bending over backwards to convince them we're a really great, chilled-out guy and totally on their wavelength, unlike most other adults our age.

We will quickly strike up a conversation about film or music, and drop references to the most recent

festival we went to, or that time we met that
famous actor at that gig. We'll always just happen
to have our cool credentials on full display, making
sure we open the front door with an eye-catching
conversation starter. 'Oh sorry, you've caught me
changing the bearings on my skateboard'; 'This
brush? I was just giving my vinyl a good going-over
– you know what static build-up's like.' Before the
youngsters can slope off, we'll have recommended
a pop-up street-art exhibition, suggested we all try
that new urban mini-golf place in town or offered
to make a playlist full of artists we think they'll
like. We might even start dropping words like
'slay', 'bro' and 'fam' into the conversation in an
only-slightly-ironic way, at which point our child
may say something like: 'Please stop talking now.'

CHAPTER TWO

Friends & Relationships

The better half: what's it like being in a relationship with an Ultra-Modern Dad?

If being an Ultra-Modern Dad sounds like hard work (and, believe us, it is), spare a thought for the people who have to live with us. It might seem that it's the children who bear the brunt of their father's fervour for all things cool (an obsession we assume will be hereditary, but usually isn't). In truth it's our wife or partner who has to put up with the most, absorbing the 'irritating' (her words) effects of our devotion to the Ultra-Modern credo like a passive smoker whose partner is a fifty-a-day man. Co-habiting with a gym freak can be exhausting – his whole life a mission to stay super-fit – but living with a middle-aged hipster, on a quest to stay super-relevant, can be more tiring. We know all this because she's told us so.

If the couple have been together for a long time, the UMD's cool crusade may – bafflingly – become more wearing with each passing year. What might have been attractive/endearing when we were in our late twenties (our Chicago deep house record collection; our Raleigh Chopper) is, she believes, starting to look a bit naff on a bloke hurtling towards his free bus pass. She might decide not to crush our feelings by telling us to our face, but our hunch is that she'll let rip when chatting to her mum friends.

It should be noted that Hipster Dads very rarely partner-up with Hipster Mums. Perhaps no home is big enough for such a pair of egos. UMD Other Halves tend to be eye-rolling, grounded, long-suffering, less financially solvent than they would have expected to be at this age, and proficient in the art of the withering put-down, most of which the UMD is possibly too self-absorbed to notice. But we know she loves us really, despite all our 'faults'.

Six things Ultra-Modern Dads and their partners argue about

1. We have nine tattoos, but not a single one referencing her or our three kids, even though our miniature schnauzer's name is emblazoned on our forearm. She has a point.

2. Belatedly, she has concerns about the fact we persuaded her to name our youngest child Ringo, even though we remember her being largely on board with the idea at the time.

3. She'd like us to go out for more meals together, and when we say we can't afford it she reminds us that we seem happy enough to pay the vast monthly instalments on our Big Green Egg barbecue.

4. She points out that we're behaving more and more like a teenage boy and that, perversely, our real teenage child is now more like the

second adult in the house when it comes to sensible conversation and financially responsible decision-making. It's a little below-the-belt when she suggests that we are ageing backwards, like a trendy Benjamin Button, 'except very much not turning into Brad Pitt'.

5. We somehow manage to spend more on beard products than she does on hair and make-up, which 'would make at least a tiny amount of sense if your beard wasn't as bedraggled as Tom Hanks's in *Castaway*'.

6. The spare room, which she repeatedly claims she had earmarked as her office, is now crammed with digital DJ controllers, guitar amps, a four-foot foosball table and other assorted online purchases, from exotic animal skulls to street art collectibles, several of which she told us in no uncertain terms we should not buy.

The friend zone: buddying up with a Hipster Dad

True fact: unlike women, all men instantly lose a large portion of their friend-making abilities the moment parenthood strikes. Once they become mothers, and despite being more knackered than they ever thought humanly possible, most women spend the next few years busily building an extensive contacts book of NCT mums, PTA pals, book-club buddies, neighbourhood WhatsAppers and Pilates partners. These extended groups can run into the hundreds, like a regional militia of mothers.

Making friends as (or with) an Ultra-Modern Dad comes much less easily. We won't be able to form a bond over babies alone. If the conversation can extend beyond children into, say, early Denis Villeneuve movies, the merits of Brutalist architecture or the surprising value of a premium

Strava account, prospective friends of UMDs are in with a shout. As a general rule, though, we are not pack animals; we certainly prefer to be the Only Hipster Dad in the Village (but not Walthamstow Village – *that* place is full of them), so we can avoid the risk of being outdone by like-minded, similarly attired competition.

But, just occasionally, a pair of UMDs will hit it off – perhaps after one of them has struck up a chat in a South American street-food queue to ask where the other acquired his vintage Belstaff biker jacket. This can go several ways: an escalating rap battle of one-upmanship, as each dad attempts to assert Alpha dominance, or the start of an intense, borderline-homoerotic bromance during which the two of them will quickly decide to quit their jobs to start a coffee business from a 1960s French delivery van. Such alliances are fragile things; witnessing one in the wild is a rare and beautiful sight, like seeing two giant pandas finally get it on.

Hipster Dads and their hipster pets

Friends are fine, but when it comes to 'special' relationships, the Ultra-Modern Dad is more likely to forge a closer bond with the animals in his life. We may claim that we acquired our family's Italian greyhound, Maine Coon cat or bearded dragon to provide companionship for little Piper and Otis, but let's not kid ourselves. Pets are an extension of our own personality, and dogs are the UMD pet of choice.

Our criteria for choosing a dog may seem superficial, but that's because they are. Temperament, grooming needs, energy levels and compatibility with small humans aren't on our list of considerations, which consists of one question: 'Does it look cool?' It may be – and usually is – the most badly behaved dog in the park, but at least it's the best-looking ('I mean, just look at the little fella in his Arket action-dog harness').

We will have insisted on getting a photogenic dog (despite our partner's protests), and by photogenic we don't mean it has doe eyes, cute ears and a glossy coat; we mean it would have looked great as part of a grainy black-and-white fashion shoot in *The Face* magazine in 2003.

A word of caution: our children may start asking why the dog is their dad's lockscreen picture, rather than a picture of them; try to avoid telling them that Mabel the podenco can't help it if she looks better in photos than they do. Bring-Your-Dog-to-the-Office Day is one of the highlights of our working year (we tend not to participate in Bring-Your-Kids-to-Work Day, for complicated reasons).

If a dog is absolutely out of the question due to a potentially fatal allergy, phobia or tenancy agreement ban, we will grudgingly consider other species, but only if they're far from obvious, and could be described as either endangered or endangering – in a trendy way. Which doesn't always go down well at home. If our kids tell us they desperately want a guinea pig, we're more likely to buy them a rat. If they plead with us for a rabbit, we might get them a corn snake. They'll defiantly call it Fluffy anyway, just to annoy us.

Five favourite Hipster Dad dog breeds

1. Whippet
2. Dobermann
3. Weimaraner
4. Border terrier
5. Siberian husky

Five favourite Mainstream Dad dog breeds

1. Cockapoo
2. Labradoodle
3. Golden retriever
4. Cavalier King Charles spaniel
5. Chihuahua

CHAPTER THREE

Music

Listen with Father: showing our kids the true musical path

If there's one thing that gets to the heart of the Ultra-Modern Dad's belief system and proves that we Still Have It, it's our passion for cool music. You may have Hipster Dad tendencies even if you don't have a Depop account, neck tattoo or Blank Street Coffee loyalty card, but if you don't have music taste that meets the required criteria, sorry, can you really call yourself a bona fide UMD?

Our music taste is much more than just a casual interest. It's a badge of honour, a sign that we belong to an elite crew. It's at the core of our being. We know our stuff, and really, really want you to know that we know. And if you don't know what we're on about, chances are you're not worth knowing.

There are two strands to our highly visible, public-facing interest in music. One, it's to convey to those who matter that we're up with the latest artists and trends. The Last Dinner Party? Been on my playlist for years, mate. ('Dad, this is their first album.') Idles? Didn't I tell you about the time I had a pee next to Jack Talbot at Ally Pally – or someone who looked quite like him? ('Yes, Dad, several times, and it's *Joe* Talbot.') Charli XCX? Duh, obviously. She's got such a distinctive sound. ('But, Dad, when I put her latest album on in the car you asked if it was Katy Perry.')

Two, it's to convey to those who matter that we've had our finger on the musical pulse for many, many years (just don't mention that time our daughter found our shameful collection of Phil Collins cassettes under the bed – much worse than discovering a cache of dirty magazines). We can not only tell you what's hot right now, but about all the music that inspired it. One of our favourite things in the world is helping our teenage offspring *understand* that their favourite artist is basically an inferior facsimile of so-and-so from the early 1990s. ('Don't you think this Fontaines D.C. ballad sounds like The Pogues? What do you mean, "*Who?*"') We're sure our kids appreciate it when we point them in the direction of something older and better, even if they don't appear to at first. This is the kind of cultural education money can't buy and they'll thank us eventually – we're sure of it. Even if for now they react with comments like, 'Why can't you just like your own stuff? You're killing my vibe.'

What does Ultra-Modern Dad music actually sound like?

Pinning down exactly which musical form or artist turns on the Ultra-Modern Dad is no simple task; our tastes are nothing if not eclectic. We are the Daddies of Disco, the Padres of Punk, the Sires of Soul, the Gurus of Grunge and the Pops of, well, Pop. We are likely to be partial to sixties girl groups, seventies reggae, eighties new wave and nineties rave, and are schooled in the classics (from Bowie to Franklin, Jagger to Byrne) – but have an aversion to actual classical in all forms. If we're serious about standing out from the crowd in a globally literate way, we may also profess a fondness for Ethiopian Afrobeat or Congolese funk. That stuff really speaks to us as a middle-aged white dude from Warwickshire.

We have a love–hate relationship with Oasis – of course we can sing every word of *Definitely Maybe*, and spent approximately 200 hours 'mastering' the guitar solo from 'Morning Glory' – but too many Mainstream Dads are into them for us to ever publicly admit we're fans. Old-school 'indie' is our heartland: the kind of songs you very much wouldn't have seen on *Top of the Pops* back in the day, or the singer with the weird haircut who frightened boring conformists (and our own parents). We've tried explaining the concept of pure-breed indie to our kids multiple times, but they don't really get it – confused by the idea of not discovering new music via TikTok.

BBC Radio 6 Music is our bellwether. While as Hipster Youths we pored over the NME for thrilling new recommendations, now our tastes are shaped and reinforced by the radio station that's built in our middle-aged-but-culturally-informed image, and largely staffed by men just like us (as old if not older, but more successful). Our Spotify choices and gig ticket purchases are sanctioned by the likes of Tom Ravenscroft and Lauren Laverne. We will have considered buying one of Self Esteem's '6 Music Dad' T-shirts but they're probably too on-the-nose. Everyone likes to feel seen, but not that much.

And yet, 6 Music can't always help us with the most important music – the songs that people a decade younger than us are into now, or the artists our teenage children are discovering. Where is a man over forty supposed to find out about those things? There's a bloke who writes for the *Guardian* who seems to know a bit, but he's in his early fifties so can he really be trusted? The Ultra-Modern Dad is aware that there are dedicated music discovery apps, but which one is best? We know social media is full of the latest music, but who to follow? In search of answers, we find ourselves conducting more online research than an Open University undergraduate.

Middle-aged merch: the art of the band T-shirt

It's somewhat heartbreaking and cruelly ironic that if there's one item of clothing in the Ultra-Modern Dad's wardrobe that best represents everything we stand for, it's also the least flattering. It's the one most likely to accentuate our moobs, beer belly and back fat. But the positives outweigh the negatives, and the band T-shirt says more about how cool we are than it does about how we really need to renew our lapsed gym membership.

We wear our band T-shirt – or, rather, one of the dozen or so band T-shirts in our closet – like a sandwich board, using it to distil crucial information (about ourselves and how we've Still Got It) in a convenient chest-mounted display of no more than fifty characters. It's our go-to shorthand method of advertising our coolness to younger members of society, of sending a message to other Hipster Dads that they have entered designated UMD territory or – like the desperate courtship display of a preening lyrebird – of attracting the sort of potential mate that gets off on the shallow signalling conveyed by an LCD Soundsystem tee.

A connoisseur of this particular craft, the UMD understands better than anyone that not all band T-shirts are created equal. In some cases it's obvious: heavy metal T-shirts are out because they seem to represent an old-fashioned masculinity that we don't subscribe to (though we have a grudging admiration for Lemmy from Motörhead). Anything goth is out because everyone knows goths were never cool (though we own several Cure albums). Nirvana, Misfits and Ramones T-shirts are out – even if we like the music – because they've been co-opted by fast-fashion brands and are bought by people who couldn't name a single one of their tunes. The more hardcore UMD will agonise over whether to buy one of The National's Sad Dads T-shirts. We know it's a manipulative marketing tactic, but that doesn't mean we're not tempted.

The Ultra-Modern Dad's guide to gigs

As already noted, the Ultra-Modern Dad is usually a solitary creature – it's easier to cement our trendy status when we're not surrounded/ threatened by other middle-aged hipsters. But there's an exception to this rule: gigs. Live music is what keeps us alive (literally: shuffling from foot to foot is the closest some UMDs get to regular exercise). The day we feel we're too old for concerts is the day to put our name down for the nearest nursing home.

Gigs are where you'll observe UMDs in their highest concentration, and it's one of Mother Nature's most remarkable sights, like pitching up at a watering hole in southern Africa and discovering a pride of lions. Is there a collective noun for Hipster Dads? Let's go with a 'bevy' – as in swans – although for gatherings of less well-maintained males, a 'bloat' may be more appropriate. As in hippos.

In the dry-ice-shrouded gloom, even close relatives would struggle to pick us out among all the other receding, bespectacled, identically dressed forty- and fifty-somethings. We're happily lost in a gently bobbing sea of slapheads, though occasionally we will be struck by the sudden realisation that everyone at concerts these days is a balding middle-aged man like us (or are we just going to the wrong gigs?).

A gig pro will position himself carefully, never too close to the stage, in case a bout of midlife moshing breaks out, or in the vicinity of a speaker – our GP reckons we're going to need a hearing aid soon, which we blame entirely on The Prodigy (Brixton Academy, 1997). We want to be not too far from the bar, although by now we have mastered the underappreciated art of carrying four wobbly pints of Red Stripe from the back of the venue to our Hipster Dad friends through a tightly packed crowd, with almost zero body contact. After years of training, we've also worked out the best point in any gig to go to the loo – the sixth-song lull, when the band inevitably opt for a slow-tempo album track. Of course, we miss the days when our youthful body didn't need a mid-gig toilet break, just as we miss the days when the dominant gig smells were weed and Silk Cut, not BO and beer farts.

Our happy place is a Pixies concert with our (admittedly unimpressed) fourteen-year-old, where we will bellow insightful comments such as: 'All the great guitar music you like? It started with this!' Look at us, we think, just a couple of cool kids in matching Doc Martens, hanging out and watching a cool band like it's the most normal thing in the world (even though one of us is thirty-two years the other's senior).

Meet me in the beer tent: fathers and festivals

If gigs are where the Ultra-Modern Dad can indulge in his favourite pastime, festivals are an outward expression of our entire personality: music, craft beer, exotic street food, glamping, the freedom to wear a cowboy hat without ridicule . . . The Hipster Dad is clearly the target demographic of the vast majority of UK festivals, whether their organisers admit it or not. UMDs are well aware of this, and we stride purposefully around those pop-up middle-class shantytowns like wise elders, planning minute-by-minute itineraries, offering tent-pitching tips to people half our age and planning routes between stages as though they were military sorties.

However, we must choose our festivals carefully: we're only forking out for an early-bird family ticket if what's on offer is a well-balanced, eclectic smorgasbord of nostalgia (the bands we liked in our early twenties) and the sort of current artists we know we *should* like if we want people to appreciate how trendy we still are.

And while we might even be thinking of upgrading to a tipi this year, we're wary of festival experiences that feel too posh, though we can definitely get on board with an on-site Co-op. We're not afraid of getting our Stan Smiths muddy, but we don't want to rough it unnecessarily. Luckily, there's a reasonable chance we know someone who knows someone who can score us a VIP lanyard. We can't decide whether we're more excited about potentially bumping into Little Simz in the backstage bar or having unfettered access to flushable loos.

We'll take the little luxuries and added benefits wherever we can, because we've experienced our fair share of festival lows over the years. Chaperoning our kids to Reading or Leeds is like a mini-break in Gomorrah, and we've vowed not to put ourselves through the terror of camping near groups of pyromaniacal teenagers again. We also have a strong dislike for festivals overtly branded as being 'family friendly', as that usually means a large contingent of Mainstream Dads and their Mainstream Kids will be present and lowering the tone, and that the line-up will be dominated by Capital FM crowd-pleasers and child-friendly, tweenybop acts. Flashpoints will ensue: 'Ethel, don't cry. I know you want to watch the CBeebies All-Stars, but Daddy thinks you'll enjoy Sleaford Mods *even more*.'

Four festivals with the highest concentration of Ultra-Modern Dads

1. **Glastonbury:** even though we like to complain about it being too corporate these days
2. **Reading:** even though we hate all the rutting teens; we're only there to stop our first-born ending up in the medical tent

3. **Boardmasters**: because we like to think we have a natural gift for watersports as well as youthful music taste
4. **Camp Bestival:** where we'll be dying inside as two adults dressed as Bluey and Bingo lead the crowd in a nursery-rhyme singalong

Four festivals Ultra-Modern Dads wouldn't be seen dead at

1. **Download** (formerly Monsters of Rock): too grungy, too rocky, too smelly
2. **Aldeburgh:** too classical, too old
3. **The Proms:** too Tory, too Radio 4
4. **Anything in Hyde Park:** too safe, too MOR, too many Mainstream Dads

Why the Hipster Dad is a
frustrated/undiscovered rock god

Part of the reason why the Ultra-Modern Dad identifies with the likes of The Strokes, Arctic Monkeys, Foo Fighters, Suede, etc. is that, bar a fickle twist of fate or two, that could have been us. ('Yes, Dad, you told us about the time you were in a band and nearly got signed by Rough Trade.') We adore our kids, but we sometimes wonder whether we'd have made the big time if fatherhood hadn't come along when it did.

But Hipster Dads never felt that having children meant it was time to put away youthful fripperies, like effects pedals. If at least one guitar isn't on semi-permanent display in a high-traffic area of the family home, we're not taking our UMD duties seriously.

How many guitars is too many? Well, how long is a piece of string? (Between 610mm and

650mm, depending on the instrument.) Yes, to the untrained ear, owning multiple expensive musical instruments that all look and sound basically the same – the way we play them, anyway – may not seem like a sound financial decision, but it's a non-negotiable. It's an effective form of Hipster Dad tax.

And, anyway, how can you put a price on the fact that our pre-teen children are our number-one fans? (For now.) Teaching our kids to play White Stripes songs and daydreaming about forming a successful family band is one of the UMD's most innocent pleasures.

Dad on the decks: am I too old to be a DJ?

Am I too old to be *anything* is not a question that troubles the Ultra-Modern Dad unduly, because if we thought about it too much our entire being would collapse like a house of cards. But the upper age limit of DJing is a subject that doesn't even cross our minds. Why would it, when there are a host of other middle-aged Hipster Dads making a nice living from making records go round and round? Norman Cook is over sixty and still packing them in. David Guetta is in his late fifties and doing just fine, thanks very much. DJ Shadow is in his second half-century and still going strong-ish.

And it's not as if the typical UMD-DJ has to worry about bad reviews in *MixMag* or losing our residency at Fabric. Most of the time we'll be spinning the decks in our garden shed to an audience of one (next door's cat). If we're feeling a little braver, we'll have volunteered to run the village-hall disco for our twelve-year-old's birthday, where our nascent beat-matching skills will go largely unappreciated. If we really want to stick our beanie hat above the parapet, we may form a DJing alliance with a fellow Hipster Dad – after one IPA too many – and offer our services to a local pub, where we'll be given a prime Sunday-night trial for our 'evening of indie bangers' (£3 on the door, £2.50 concessions).

The only thing worrying us about the whole arrangement is our failing eyesight, the professional curse of the middle-aged would-be DJ. It's hard enough to read the words on an album sleeve in dim light when you've got early-onset night blindness, let alone figure out where to drop the needle. There's a reason why those Orbital blokes wear their fancy head torches.

Midlife mixtapes: pay attention to my playlist

Today's mixtape may be digital – an iPhone playlist – but it's still a highly effective method of coaching the next generation to ensure they know their right and wrong, euphonically speaking. Who better to learn from than the man who came of age in the golden age of mixtapes (as in, actual C90 cassettes)?

Starting them young is crucial, as is reducing their exposure to crap music wherever possible: once peer pressure and social media has opened their ears to Olivia Rodrigo and SZA, it can be a fierce battle to get them back on the straight and narrow. Gene Gallagher, son of Ultra-Modern Dad archetype Liam, once admitted that 'none of us grew up with pop', because Dad 'didn't want us listening to Justin Bieber or One Direction, none of that malarkey'. Instead, the little Gallaghers were fed a full-fat UMD diet of The Who and The Beatles. And quite right, too.

Long car journeys provide the ideal backdrop for these character-building music lessons, with every family trip providing an opportunity to inculcate an appreciation of The Flaming Lips, De La Soul or Kate Bush in the impressionable minds of young passengers. It's important to stand firm in the face of resistance or complaints, or comments like: 'My friend Sophie says her dad thinks Bruno Mars is better than David Bowie.' It's also essential to retain full control of the Apple CarPlay settings until the children of the family are at least fourteen and can be trusted with such adult responsibilities.

It's all about saving one's children from a fate worse than death: having bad taste. The moment a child tells a Hipster Dad that they're now really into the Andrew Lloyd Webber back catalogue will haunt us for the rest of our days.

Five bands/artists Ultra-Modern Dads love

1. The National
2. Charli XCX
3. Radiohead
4. Gorillaz
5. English Teacher

Five bands/artists Ultra-Modern Dads hate

1. Coldplay
2. Coldplay
3. Coldplay
4. Coldplay
5. Coldplay

A word on (Hipster) Dad dancing

When we had more hair (and oh, kids, *what* a head of hair), we could swush it from side to side, and back to front, at various tempos, from Nirvana-fast to shoegaze-slow. At one point in the early noughties we even mastered a few rudimentary Northern Soul moves, but now our knees have gone.

These days, we know how silly a slightly overweight balding middle-aged man dancing looks. Thus: the true Hipster Dad doesn't dance. Under any circumstances.

CHAPTER FOUR

Style

Still got fits: dressing the Ultra-Modern Dad

According to countless men's magazines and newspaper fashion editors, deciding what to wear as a middle-aged man can be a 'minefield', and they invariably suggest following certain 'rules'. Keep it classic, they warn. Be sensible and don't scare the horses. Avoid big logos and prominent branding. Wear muted colours at all times. And, for the love of God, don't ever try to dress like a teenager.

To which the Ultra-Modern Dad says: what a crock of hooey. Such 'expert' advice might be fine for Mainstream Dads, but for the UMD this approach to getting dressed is beyond boring – and just plain wrong.

We have our own set of guidelines, thanks very much. Roughly a third of our wardrobe will be made up of what could loosely be described as 'workwear' (even though the only manual labour we're capable of consists of occasionally oiling the chain on our vintage racing bike). Heritage brands feature heavily, especially ones that started life fifty-plus years ago making overalls for oil-riggers, donkey jackets for navvies or hobnail boots for coal miners. Our favourite labels tend to combine a blue-collar ethos with blue-chip prices.

We are also a walking example of the irrepressible midlife male craving for Batman-esque levels of wearable utility: jackets with too many pockets, trousers with pointless functionality. (Hammer loop? Don't mind if I do.) All of this makes us feel just-manly-enough but not obnoxiously macho, and helps balance out the emasculating effects of pushing a buggy.

If workwear is one of our fashion pillars, another is streetwear. Even if we weren't exactly champion breakdancers in our youth (and we most definitely weren't), we'd like people to believe we *could* be guys with a b-boy past, or who still bear a few skateboarding scars (nope) and whose graffiti tags can still be seen in the ungentrified corners of our hometown (absolutely not). Which is why you might often see us dressed in sweats and joggers, sneakers or sliders, hoping to convey an image that looks more Beastie Boys than *Benefits Street*.

Several pieces in our sartorial arsenal will offer a nod to our nineties/noughties heyday (indie-kid Breton tops, Doc Martens) and we might have doggedly held on to a favourite denim jacket that is now impossible to button up. But with other pieces we'll co-opt trends from Gen Z, including items we weren't exactly fans of the first time round, such as fleeces and cargo pants (our kids snort when we refer to them as 'combat trousers').

Despite our age, we feel perfectly at home browsing the rails of Urban Outfitters – although the other customers assume we're elderly store detectives – or scrolling through ASOS, even though we end up wondering why eighteen-year-old boys are so very muscly these days.

Our clothes obsession leaves our better halves rolling their eyes when another END. Clothing parcel hits the doormat: 'Aren't I supposed to be the one with the secret shopping habit?' Our teenage children react to our purchases with a mix of bewilderment and horror, especially when we misjudge or take things too far. 'If Paul Mescal can carry off short shorts, why can't I?' 'Because he's *literally half your age*, Dad, and doesn't have knee fat.' But when we get it right the pleasure is immeasurable. The day we catch our teenage sons wearing our Harrington jacket is one of the happiest of our parenting life.

Style

We credit ourselves with a Savile Row-level understanding of which clothes are flattering, and which are likely to knock a few years off our real age when we're out in public. We'll own at least three baggy hoodies for this purpose, and viewed from the back while wearing one we could probably pass for one of our teenage sons' mates, in a dark alley at least. Although the unfortunate trade-off is that when we turn round we inadvertently recreate the final harrowing scene from *Don't Look Now*.

Three of the most essential items in the Hipster Dad's wardrobe

1. **Overshirts galore.** We hate the word 'shacket' but have one for every day of the week – boxy, heavyweight, durable, forgiving – they are our 365-day go-to for smart-casual dressing. Not that we'd ever use the words 'smart-casual'. Our partners swear at least three of them are not only similar but literally identical, but our number-one clothes-buying principle is that if you like something you should buy three versions of it, just to be on the safe side.

2. **T-shirts. But not any old T-shirts.** And not just band T-shirts either. We'll also have T-shirts with printed images of film and TV characters, cool or ironic, probably from the 1970s or 80s. We may own a classic print, like the 'New York City' top John Lennon wore

in 1974, or a vintage football jersey for an obscure European or South American team with a cool name. ('Come on, you Go Ahead Eagles!')

3. **Vacation shirts.** Summer's answer to winter's overshirt, these are short-sleeved shirts with flat, open collars and bold patterns, and unparalleled when it comes to disguising middle-aged spreads. The vibe is Tony Soprano at the family barbecue, but in the wrong hands the effect can be more Eric Bristow at the oche, so proceed with caution.

Fashion crises: what not to wear

There are certain items that the UMD wouldn't be seen dead in because they're for Mainstream Dads only: e.g. brown footwear of any kind, or quarter-zip knits (aka 'Tory jumpers'), as favoured by bankers on dress-down Fridays. But it's not always so simple. Sometimes a piece of clothing can go from the height of trendiness to highly Hipster-Dad-inappropriate overnight, so it's important to know that what's cool today could be deeply uncool tomorrow, and when to bail out of a trend. For example: vintage-style navy-blue French chore jackets were practically the compulsory uniform for UMDs before the Covid pandemic. But as soon as disgraced health secretary and walking midlife crisis Matt Hancock was photographed wearing one, they instantly became as unfashionable as Boris Johnson's running shorts. Ditto Adidas Sambas, which had been a nailed-on Hipster Dad signifier for years until Rishi Sunak wore them in an interview to promote government tax policy. When fellow Mainstream Dad Keir Starmer then quipped that he was more of a Gazelles man, Hipster Dads made a beeline for charity shops to offload their Adidas.

Hipster Dad fashion brands	vs	Mainstream Dad fashion brands
Carhartt		Next
New Balance		SuperDry
Dickies		Thomas Pink
Supreme		Polo Ralph Lauren
Patagonia		White Stuff
Vans		Gant
Fred Perry		Barbour
Stüssy		M&S
Fjällräven		Ted Baker
Red Wing		Reiss

The finishing touches:
accessorising the Hipster Dad

Footwear

If you're unsure whether you're dealing with
a genuine Ultra-Modern Dad, or one who just
happens to be married to someone who is good
at birthday presents, there's one way to know for
sure: look down.

UMD dressing often starts from the feet up. Is
he brave/foolhardy enough to wear white socks?
Usually a Hipster Dad giveaway. Are his boots or
trainers in pristine condition? Almost certainly
a Hipster Dad. Flip-flops in September? Classic
Hipster Dad behaviour.

In bad weather, we'll probably be sporting a pair
of chunky, overengineered hiking boots. They'll
boast 'Goodyear welted construction' (we don't

know what that means but know it's good), will be waterproof, snowproof and active-volcano-proof, endorsed by Tibetan Sherpas and the SAS, with steel toes and optional crampon attachments. We will mostly wear them to drop our daughters off at Brownies or to walk the dog.

In summer, we might be in a pair of bright yellow Crocs, because young people thought David Hockney's pair looked cool (what they meant was, it was a cool look *if you happen to be David Hockney*).

Year-round, we will have three or four pairs of trainers in rotation at any given time, and we will deem them appropriate for any occasion: work, pub, football match, even the odd wedding. Everything about them will be gloriously retro, apart from the price. We think – and tell our partners, unconvincingly – that spaffing £100 on footwear is actually a wise financial investment: 'You don't understand the market. These are limited-edition New Balance 990s – they'll be worth double in five years.' The trainers will be practical and comfortable, which is a bonus because we will probably have developed fallen arches and a recurrence of an ingrown toenail. They will also exactly fit the definition of what young people would call 'dad trainers', which we may fail to understand are cutting-edge trendy when worn by someone under twenty-five, but lose all of their ironic appeal when worn by an actual middle-aged man like us.

We will have spotted them on TikTok or being sported by a colleague half our age. 'Look at us!' we'll say in the office corridor, casually, 'Trainer buddies!' (The young colleague will mysteriously never be seen in them ever again.)

Headwear

Unlike most of what the Hipster Dad wears, our headwear choices are informed by genuinely practical reasoning: we need something to cover our big balding heads. Something to keep the heat off in summer (why did no one warn us that we needed to apply SPF50 up there, and that head sunburn is the most painful type of all?), and to keep the winter elements at bay.

Even if, all things considered, we think we look pretty good most of the time, and could pass for half a decade below our real age, we know our greying, thinning, fast-degenerating hair is letting the side down. It's the reason why, in all cultures across the centuries, men have worn hats.

But not any old hat will do. Flat caps are risky – if our faces are too grizzled and saggy, we'll end up looking like a member of the *Last of the Summer*

Wine cast. More knowingly trendy baker-boy caps are a safer bet, if the desired effect is 'Tommy Shelby goes to a soft-play centre'. Most Hipster Dads will opt for a colourful beanie (winter) or baseball/trucker cap (summer). The beanie should be teeny and, for that matter, weeny – above the ear, never over. The cap should feature a heritage logo, or some sort of rugged, American outdoorsy branding, like 'Bob's Sawmill, Nebraska, 1932'.
A vintage-style cycling cap is also acceptable. Score additional UMD points if it has never actually been worn for cycling.

Eyewear

It's not just our hair follicles that are failing us; so is our eyesight. However, Ultra-Modern Dads take this as an opportunity to explore our trendy eyewear options. Unlike the Mainstream Dad, Hipster Dads *want* other people to notice our glasses, from across a crowded room if possible, and to know that we're fully owning our age-related astigmatism and presbyopia. Yes, I am going blind, we say, but I still know what looks good. We may not have satisfactorily answered such nagging questions as 'Are super-chunky, Michael-Caine-in-the-sixties-style frames still cool if my lenses are thicker than the bottom of beer bottles?' or 'Am I possibly too old for aviators, especially if I need bifocals?', but that won't stop us.

As a midlifer, the Hipster Dad will also understand the importance – and growing necessity – of a Really Good Pair of Sunglasses. Not a practical-but-dull Mainstream Dad pair, picked up for a tenner at a motorway service station, but a pair that conveys the essence of our cooler-than-the-rest-of-you personalities. Unlike Mainstream Dads, we will often wear our shades when it isn't sunny, including indoors, not least because they're good for concealing our knackered eye bags and generally bloodshot demeanour. They also help us avoid making eye contact with Mainstream Dads at after-school pick-up.

The delicate craft of Hipster Dad hair management

Most UMDs at one time, pre-children, set great store by their hair. In our youth, a haircut wasn't just a haircut – it was an opportunity to point to a photograph of an achingly hip American guitarist or French actor from the 1970s and say to a £10 barber: 'Could you make it look like that, please?' By our late twenties, we will have settled on what we felt was our forever style, cool but timeless, a look to grow into as we aged. But then something almost imperceptible happened. Our hairlines looked pointier and distinctly V-shaped. Our foreheads got bigger. As Harry Hill once observed, it was taking us longer and longer to wash our faces. Baldness was knocking at the door, like a depilating Grim Reaper.

Of course, because inside our own heads we are still and always will be twenty-seven, we often forget that our outward appearance is that of a much older, balder man, and it's always a deeply wounding experience when we catch a glimpse of our bald spots in changing-room mirrors, doorbell cameras and holiday snaps.

If our hair is thinning badly, we will employ a creative combination of comb work and wax/ gel/spray/powder to conjure an optical illusion of hirsuteness. Sadly, rain and wind can destroy our handiwork in an instant, pulling back the rug (figuratively and literally) and leaving us looking like Donald Trump in a tornado.

If the damage is minimal (for now), we may stay loyal to our receding rockabilly quiff or glad-to-be-grey mod cut. But there will likely come a time when it's all got to go. When that day inevitably arrives, we will pray to all the gods that we'll be left looking more like Stanley Tucci than a naked mole-rat.

We may be one of the lucky few to retain a thick and luscious head of hair well into midlife, but even that is not without its dangers. We may feel tempted to experiment with young men's hair trends, like curly mop-tops with a high fade, but the look of horror on the faces of members of our household when we say, 'How do you think I'd look if . . . ?' should be enough to jolt us back to reality. While we genuinely believe we can do or wear almost anything that a man half our age can, in our heart of hearts we know that mullets are forever off limits.

It's not all bad news and the universe is not completely unfair: what it takes away with one hand, it giveth with the other. Quite often, when Ultra-Modern Dads lose the ability to grow hair on the top of our heads, our ability to sprout it from other parts of our bodies ramps up several gears (though sadly this includes knuckles, ears and other extremities: we may sometimes feel we are turning into the Burt Reynolds of toe hair). This means that, in middle age, we are unimpeachably at our Facial Hair Prime. The patchy, disappointing beard days of our youth are behind us and we can now grow a proper, full-bodied moustache. In moments of self-doubt, we know that this is one area in which our teenage son or daughter's boyfriend cannot yet defeat us.

A word on tattoos

The Hipster Dad is old enough to remember the old tattoo rules. Less was more, and one was almost always enough. The accepted templates were either Polynesian tribal or Celtic spiritual – or, for the hardcore, a thin band of barbed wire round an upper limb. Acceptable locations included – and, in fact, were strictly limited to – upper arms and shoulder blades. Anything more than that singled you out as a member of society's dangerous fringes. Anything below the waist was frankly weird.

The Mainstream Dad still thinks all of the above holds true, but the UMD has moved with the times. We've clocked all the inked-up celebrity chefs and Premier League footballers. We've seen Harry Styles with his top off (on our daughter's bedroom wall). And while part of us understands that getting a new tattoo is something that shouldn't be on the agenda past the age of forty, like starting vaping (guilty as charged), our hipster brain knows what's what. We adhere to the new rules: fewer than five tattoos is no longer enough. At least two of them should be visible at all times, including while wearing a winter coat. They should be located on an unexpected part of the body, designed to make observers think, 'Christ, I bet that was painful.' And they should look like a random, mismatched assortment of drunken doodles on the back of a toilet door, hand-drawn and hastily applied in a Siberian prison by a terrifying brute called Boris, not by a millennial in the Home Counties called Hugo. If anyone asks, we will obviously say we had them done in our late teens.

Of course, we have a very different attitude to body art when our eighteen-year-old returns from a Greek island with a small tattoo of a fish on her ribcage. We'll smile and compliment it, but will be quietly devastated.

CHAPTER FIVE

Food & Drink

Feeding the Ultra-Modern Dad

Fact: Mainstream Dads aren't really interested in food – at least, not the preparation of it. They might have strong opinions on the optimal texture of a roast potato or what constitutes the perfect fry-up, but the only occasions when they're likely to take charge of the cooking is during barbecue season (i.e. two weekends a year) or when it's time to make the Christmas gravy.

Ultra-Modern Dads, on the other hand, are our households' designated chefs (self-appointed), 365 days of the year, from Saturday brunches to elaborate feasts for friends. In part, we are driven by the nagging voice in our heads that says, 'Do not turn into your own father' – a man incapable of boiling an egg – and by the compulsion to be a thoroughly modern bloke who Does Things Around the House Without Having to be Asked. But we have also been inspired by a host of famous, rock-star chefs – Jamie, Gordon, Marco, Heston, Yotam and co. – who, back in the noughties, convinced a large portion of men like us that making food is dead cool, actually.

It's widely accepted that most men over the age of thirty-five yearn for a Man Cave of their own, but what the UMD understands is that there's no need to dig out the cellar or damp-proof the shed, as a Mainstream Dad would do. We will simply execute a non-hostile takeover of the family kitchen. The centre of the Ultra-Modern Dad universe, the kitchen is our fiefdom, our domain, our nerve centre, bunker, safe space and dream factory. If you'll find us anywhere, you'll find us there, magicking up another exotic masterpiece, and happily alone (we don't respond well to offers of assistance or well-meaning criticism: sous chefs need not apply).

What are we cooking?, you may ask (our families
certainly do, anxiously). As men who have
moved with the times and have our fingers on
the culinary pulse, we have firm views on what
will and won't appear on our menus. Yes, we'll
be taking our wives and children on authentic
gastronomic tours of Asia, South America and
North Africa, from the comfort of their own home,
the lucky devils. Yes, a handful of British pub-grub
classics will make occasional appearances, but
only if we can give them an idiosyncratic UMD
spin, with the addition of a surprising hipster
ingredient or two – you should *totally* try our nduja
carbonara. No, we won't be making anything
that is likely to meet with the approval of Delia
Smith, Mary Berry or their trad disciples. And,
no, we don't do desserts, so don't even ask (we
think all puddings are a bit soppy). Gammon is
also permanently off the menu due to a) its 1970s

connotations, and b) the word being a bit close to the bone for men of our age.

When constructing our families' weekly meal plan, we begin with a question: if a recipe can be sourced entirely at our nearest Sainsbury's Local, how good can it be, really? Where possible, each dish should include at least one ingredient bought from a specialist online retailer. We have developed a minor obsession with these websites as we doggedly work our way through the Dishoom cookbook, and now roughly 50 per cent of our fridge consists of open jars of obscure artisan condiments. Several kitchen cupboards are also devoted to foodstuffs we bought once and used a teaspoon of in a single recipe.

Cookbooks are now a rarity when it comes to UMD meal prep. These days, we're fully digital. We get most of our recipes from twenty-somethings on TikTok rather than Nigel Slater, which our other halves find slightly tragic. And we spend a disproportionate amount of time watching YouTube tutorials on fermentation and breadmaking. Our efforts to keep our sourdough starter alive against the odds deserve a Pride of Britain award, even though we haven't made a loaf since the second Covid lockdown.

Do our families appreciate the superhuman efforts we go to in order to broaden their epicurean horizons? Of course they don't. If our youngest would eat a vegetable other than peas, that would be an achievement – but that won't stop us piling their plates with Japanese seaweed and daikon. It breaks our hearts to hear our six-year-old say: 'But, Daddy, I don't like gochujang. It makes my tongue hurt.'

Things you'll find in the Ultra-Modern Dad's fridge

- Tahini
- Miso
- Chilli crisp
- Bone broth (home-made)
- An offensively pungent cheese that has contaminated everything in the vicinity

And things you won't (but you'll find them in the Mainstream Dad's fridge)

- Salad cream
- Pork pie
- Mild Cheddar
- Iceberg lettuce
- Ready meals

Why it's all about the kit
(that we can't really afford)

With the onset of middle age, the stresses of work and the pressures of parenting, many men start to crave an expensive new toy as reward for having made it this far in life relatively intact. But while the Mainstream Dad might dream of a Range Rover, the Ultra-Modern Dad dreams of a Rangemaster. The Mainstream Dad wants a four-wheel drive and twin exhausts. The Ultra-Modern Dad wants at least six gas burners (only two of them ever likely to be used) and a double oven. Our midlife fantasy sports car is just a really big cooker.

And that's only the start. One of the reasons we love cooking so much is the opportunity it presents to surround ourselves with a vast amount of largely unnecessary equipment, from imported semi-legal Japanese knives, to those disposable black nitrile gloves that all the manly chefs wear on Instagram. Where possible, the kit should be solid, sturdy and Michelin-star standard. Pots and pans should be too heavy for our children to lift (even if that effectively disqualifies them from washing-up duty). There's more cast iron in our kitchens than in the Clifton Suspension Bridge.

The more likely our equipment is to put us in A&E, the better it is. For the last two Christmases, we will have unsuccessfully lobbied our partners for one of those Iberico legs of pork on a wooden stand – not because we love Spanish ham especially, but because there's a 50 per cent chance of losing a thumb while carving it.

We own an assortment of deadly-looking, sharp-edged tools that resemble implements you'd find in the hands of a Vietnam War field surgeon. At least half of them look like they'd breach the 2019 Offensive Weapons Act. Our wives will have installed roughly 200 child locks in the kitchen and all but banned our children from entering the room unaccompanied.

Under interrogation, we can argue convincingly that each and every item, however obscure it may seem, was an essential purchase. Yes, of course we need a pair of lobster pliers. All kitchens should have a pair of gnocchi paddles. No, a sous vide machine is not a monumental waste of money. Our scientific approach to gastronomy means we can fully justify the purchase of gadgets like a top-of-the-range digital thermometer or the sort of high-end electronic scales Walter White would fully endorse.

We will occasionally take our cooking skills outdoors, and who can forget the time we tried to build our own pizza oven in the garden – though it's been out of action after setting fire to the neighbour's fence, and is now occupied by a family of parasite-infested foxes. We are not (quite) too snobbish to use a barbecue, but will resist our children's requests for sausages and chicken drumsticks in favour of smoky, low-and-slow Texan-style extravaganzas that take twelve hours to cook and aren't ready until way past our kids' bedtime.

Bean there, done that:

the Hipster Dad's guide to coffee

While you might sometimes find us on the sofa at
home, sipping a cup of Tetley as we flick through
the *New York Times* cooking app, coffee is the
Ultra-Modern Dad's go-to liquid refreshment.
Caffeine is in our blood, at levels which concern
our doctors. ('Twelve cups a day might not be
causing your high blood pressure, but it certainly
isn't helping, and a man of *your age* needs to be
careful.') But our addiction stretches far beyond
the jumpstarts – it's the rituals and aesthetics of
coffee that have got us hooked.

True, we are the oldest amateur baristas in town,
but we're also among the best (as well we should
be, considering the cost of those latte art courses
we did). We know our ristretto from our lungo,
obviously, and we are experts on flavour profiles

and roast types, and won't let people forget it. Naturally, we're the kind of men who grind our own beans – which grinds our partners' gears, for some reason – and we know better than most that Ethiopian beans have floral and berry notes, while beans from Guatemala have more of a chocolatey sweetness, duh. That's what we read, anyway – we can't actually taste the difference.

We find it harder to justify the cost of the metre-long, stainless steel, industrial-grade coffee machine that's taken centre stage in our kitchen, like some sort of out-of-proportion art installation. We insisted that it would pay for itself within a year or two (make that ten), but we still buy at least five oat flat whites a week from the trendy coffee truck near our office. And of course we barely know how to use it. In our defence, the manual was over 200 pages long.

In case of emergencies, we won't travel anywhere without our portable AeroPress, for caffeine hits on the go. ('It's your version of an epipen, if epipens were for dickheads,' our partners tell us. When our kids ask, 'Why is Dad so stressed?', it's because he's on his eighth cortado of the day, and it's only 2 p.m.

When it comes to visiting cafés, we have strict criteria: if they don't serve flax milk, bake a top-notch pastel de nata and sell their own hemp tote bags, we'll be cycling on by. We have a pathological contempt for chain coffee shops, as well as cafés with a disproportionate number of mums, pushchairs and noisy toddlers (we believe the correct proportion to be: zero). We're more likely to be taking our own offspring to kid-free places where every other customer is in their mid-twenties. Believing them to be more our 'tribe' than our fellow local parents, we will strike up conversations with the bored staff about bean-harvesting procedures, whether they like it or not.

Do our children think our coffee obsession is cool? Well, if they're under seven they ask for a babyccino (frothy milk with a dusting of cocoa). If they're impressionable tweens, they'll have a sip of one of our famed brews, pull a face and not understand what the fuss is about. If they're old enough to have even a vague sense of how much money we're throwing at our addiction, they'll think we've lost our marbles.

Dining out with an Ultra-Modern Dad

Before we had kids, there was a blissful, too-short window of food-related hedonism during which we were able to afford to go to all of the latest, trendiest establishments. We didn't mind places with no-booking policies that made us queue in the rain, or which were so fashionable they only had available tables after 9.45 p.m. We were young, breezy and child-free, with the emphasis on *free*. Then, children came along and now we only eat out in places with disposable, colour-in paper placemats on every table. Or places that hand out garishly branded balloons, so that we must effectively announce to the whole world on our way home that we have given up on life. Or places that have alarmingly and mysteriously sticky floors and where the ambient sound is of at least two toddlers having Fukushima-level meltdowns. If the pram in the hall is the enemy of good art, then the highchair in the restaurant is surely the enemy of good food. The one good thing about these places is that at least there's zero chance of bumping into one of our cool, millennial, non-parent colleagues.

Of all the phrases associated with parenthood that make the Hipster Dad die inside, 'Would you like to see the children's menu?' occupies the top spot. How are we supposed to encourage Arlo and Pearl to broaden their culinary horizons when the only options are chicken nuggets or spag bol? God knows we've tried to get our fussy ingrate children to embrace dim sum and poke bowls (when all they really want is a Nando's), but we are inevitably met with the sort of stubborn denial normally only witnessed in SAS 'resistance to torture' training. That is, of course, until our children are having a meal with friends or their friends' families, after which they will come home and cheerfully boast that, actually, they now really love olives, anchovies, squid, asparagus, kale, chillies, couscous or one of the hundreds of other food items that led to a high-volume family argument in a chain restaurant, followed by a 'quiet word' from the waiters.

UMD/IPA: the Hipster Dad in the pub

If coffee shops are the Ultra-Modern Dad's daytime refuge, the pub is where you'll find us of an evening. Not every evening, of course. We know our middle-aged limits and getting hammered is now a very rare occurrence. We've reached the stage of life where we favour quality over quantity. And although we typically drink expensive craft beer from local breweries, with street-art branding and seemingly named by a not-very-witty fourteen-year-old boy, we grudgingly accept that it is going to give us a chronic, week-long hangover and do something to our lower digestive tract that we'd rather not talk about outside the sacramental seal of a GP's surgery. So we drink in moderation. Not least because our beers of choice taste like fermented pond water.

As with cafés, you won't just find us in any old pub. We have standards. We have fully embraced the taproom movement and love nothing more than hanging out in damp, cold disused railway arches, and chatting to the bearded millennials who work in them about how we're thinking of getting into the craft-beer business ourselves.

We're not a fan of wanky gastropubs (just restaurants with a few hand pumps, not fooling anyone) or old-fashioned CAMRA-endorsed boozers, because they tend to be full of (and smell of) old farts. We don't like wine bars because we don't really care for wine – it's more of a Mainstream Dad beverage (fact: the UMD does not own a wine fridge or cellar and cannot talk knowledgeably about grape varieties, because wine knowledge is blatantly a sign of boring old age). We like to check out the latest trendy spots, although we don't find it amusing when doormen sarcastically ask us if they can see some ID. Negronis tend to be our cocktails of choice, though we like to think we make better ones

ourselves (the Hipster Dad home bar is definitely
A Thing).

It breaks our hearts that our teenage kids and
their friends only drink in the local 'Spoon's,
because it's all they can afford. We're still haunted
by the days when our own dads would leave us in
the car outside their local with a packet of crisps
and a bottle of pop. UMDs, on the other hand,
desperately want to be in the pub with our own
children once they reach a certain age (and that
age is eighteen months). We will have introduced
them to alcohol gently when they were pre-teens
– we tell ourselves this will give them a healthier
relationship with booze, like the French, and that
it demonstrates what chilled-out modern guys
we are. A few years later, we'll be getting drunk
with them at a festival and feeling jealous of their
ability to keep going far beyond midnight – and
their lack of hangovers. We'll pat ourselves on
the back in the knowledge that moments like

this prove what cool dads we are, and that we have successfully assimilated ourselves into the social milieu of the generation beneath us. But if we think about it for too long we might come to the conclusion that they're just using us for free drinks.

CHAPTER SIX

Work & Leisure

The Ultra-Modern Dad at work

While young hipsters are earning a crust at artisan
bakeries or bike repair shops, Hipster Dads need to
do something more remunerative for a living – all
that Japanese denim won't pay for itself, and nor
will the mortgage. But what sort of jobs do Hipster
Dads do? Almost anything, it turns out. Yes, we'd
love to have been a graphic designer, film producer
or festival organiser, or at the very least some
sort of digital consultant in one of the creative
industries (how hard can that be?). We still dream
about opening our own second-hand record
shop, and we've been giving serious thought to
retraining as a stand-up comedian. But we now
accept that most jobs are more boring than that.
And as long as working in insurance/accountancy/
sales helps fund our hipster lifestyle, that's the
main thing.

Truth is, there's a Hipster Dad in most offices, if you know how to spot us. We'll be the ones doing lunchtime yoga four times a week, clearly thinking we're the best in the class and talking loudly about it afterwards. We'll be drinking kombucha and matcha lattes at our desks, bringing in home-made, potently fragrant packed lunches made with exotic ingredients, and asking colleagues if they'd like a bite. We'll be the ones reminding our twenty-something team when it's half-price cocktails night at our local (none of them drink) or trying to gather the young troops to try out that new pétanque-themed bar in town. (It kills us when we find out they've already been, without us.) You'll hear us complimenting our younger male colleagues on their bags, coats and shirts, asking everyone which festivals they're going to this year, if they've heard the new Waxahatchee track or got tickets for Chappell Roan – and only occasionally mispronouncing artists' names.

We'll try not to resent having bosses who are considerably younger than us, though we're fairly certain our colleagues think we're in our thirties (but we probably wouldn't want to know what they really think).

Hipster Dad hobbies

We take them far too seriously to use a flippant word like 'hobby', but if the Cambridge Dictionary definition is anything to go by – 'an activity one does for pleasure when not working' – we have them coming out of our ears. The Ultra-Modern Dad is nothing if not a pleasure-seeking creature, and much of that pleasure comes from knowing we're cooler than everyone else.

Our pastimes extend from sofa-based to the sort of sporty physical activity that our life insurance company really ought to know about. We're not sure it counts as a hobby, but we spend a huge amount of time on TikTok and Instagram (scrolling for cooking tips, modern architecture porn and clips of other Hipster Dads discussing the stories behind lesser-known Radiohead songs), even though we frequently lecture our kids on the dangers of smartphone addiction.

We like to tell people we're looking to invest in more street art, though we're haunted by the experience of buying a piece in a pub ten years ago that a fellow Hipster Dad convinced us was a genuine Banksy, but was actually bashed out by a local A-level student.

One of our favourite weekend activities is dragging our kids on demos: anti-war, anti-student loans, pro-refugees, anti-water pollution or whatever the *Guardian* is up in arms about this week. Terrified of being out of touch, or becoming one of those people who turn into Tories as soon as their hair goes grey, we're determined to be on the right side of history when it comes to society's big calls, especially around diversity and climate change. Our children are significantly less bothered, especially if a march to Downing Street interferes with their Saturday morning lie-in.

We're well aware that our own fathers didn't have hobbies at all – they had DIY. This is very much

not a leisure option for the Ultra-Modern Dad.
Which is not to say that we're useless with a
toolbox – it's simply that traditional DIY is out,
and crafting is in. We can't for the life of us
unblock a sink or install a toilet seat, but if you
need someone to knock up a coffee table out
of driftwood, or convert the box room into a
soundproofed music studio we're your guys.

Play hard: Ultra-Modern Dads and their toys

Some fathers put away childish things when they reach adulthood, but a large part of the Hipster Dad's brain will be permanently thirteen years old. Call it an endearing wiring defect. We love nothing more than getting down on the living-room rug to play with our kids' toys – whether or not our kids are playing. Show us the lid of a Scalextric or Subbuteo box and we'll dissolve into a Proustian flashback, tearfully reliving our pre-puberty prime. To say we love LEGO more than our own kids do is no understatement, but that's largely because we insist on only buying them the hardcore adult sets (1:100 scale Camp Nou stadium or Guggenheim Museum; Land Rover Classic Defender with partially functioning internal combustion engine). Then there are the beloved adult toys we can't live without – the grown-up gadgets that thrill and delight us, from the guitar capo Johnny Marr once recommended in a YouTube tutorial to an eBay-acquired vintage Super 8 camera, perfect for those arty, sepia-tinted family home movies, which our partner says make our camping holidays look like *The Blair Witch Project*.

The Ultra-Modern Dad likes to think he grew up in the heyday of video games – and we won't let our kids forget it. We've tried to persuade them that the computer games of our own youth were as-good-if-not-better than the £50-a-pop rip-offs everyone plays now, but whenever we show them clips on YouTube they just laugh at the shonky 16-bit graphics and crummy sound effects, the little heathens.

Luckily, age hasn't dimmed our highly developed gaming skills, and nowhere is our competitive streak more evident than when challenging our kids to an intense round of Splatoon or Rocket League. Despite wails of protest, we find it impossible to dial down our naturally elite abilities to match our children's Year 4 skill levels – the thrill of victory is just too powerful. Once someone hands us a Mario Kart steering wheel, we turn into a raging Max Verstappen.

What we might not understand is that our victories will be fleeting, our supremacy short-lived. The terrible day is coming – sooner than we realise – when our children will be able to defeat us at literally every single game (usually around age ten). Few things in life will make us feel as old.

Silver hair, silver screen:
the Hipster Dad viewing guide

Among our potential specialist subjects for a
TV quiz show (we think we'd be brilliant), the
Ultra-Modern Dad's top contender is movies.

We're certain that we could have been a leading
professional film critic if we'd known the right
people in our twenties. But that doesn't stop
us spending a huge amount of time writing
Letterboxd reviews no one will read. In the
absence of a more appreciative audience, we
share our razor-sharp opinions and encyclopaedic
film knowledge with our children. As with
music, we consider it an essential part of our
duty as modern parents to impart our cultural
wisdom, and fill our children's brains with a deep
understanding of the collective oeuvres of the
Coen Brothers, Scorsese, Kubrick and David Lynch.

We'll start them young: while their friends are innocently plonked in front of Minions and Tinker Bell films, our offspring will be sitting through back-to-back Studio Ghibli marathons, enhanced by our highly detailed commentaries on magical realism and the history of Japanese anime. We will attempt a Disney ban (doomed) and will make sure they're exposed to early De Niro and Nicholson masterpieces before they've graduated from primary school. We'll encourage them to watch the original Star Wars trilogy, but bar them from watching any of the others, and be clear that *Dark Star*, *Silent Running* and the first *Alien* are far superior space films anyway (although the latter gives our ten-year-old recurring nightmares, oops).

We may soften our tactics as the children get older, bonding with our pre-teens over the Spiderverse films, *LEGO Batman* and the Tim Burton back catalogue. And once our kids hit their mid/late teens, we will suggest cinema trips to see the latest Timothée Chalamet or Zendaya dramas, or a bit of A24 arthouse horror. We're baffled when they decline.

Five of the best cinematic UMDs

1. John McClane (Bruce Willis),
   Die Hard

2. Han Solo (Harrison Ford),
   Star Wars: The Force Awakens

3. Michael Corleone (Al Pacino),
   The Godfather Part II

4. Joseph Cooper (Matthew McConaughey),
   Interstellar

5. Furious Styles (Laurence Fishburne),
   Boyz n the Hood

The grand tour: Hipster Dads on holiday

When it comes to vacations, Ultra-Modern Dads will do everything in our power to resist the convenient pull of the package holiday. Even we are not immune to the temptation of kids' clubs and all-you-can-eat breakfasts, but we're all too aware that Center Parcs, Thomas Cook and TUI are pitched squarely at Mainstream Dads, and we know we can do better than that.

Instead of sitting around a pool with a hundred toddlers and their parents, we'd much rather be dragging our families around the filming locations from our favourite movies ('Why aren't you more excited, everyone? It's the dam Pierce Brosnan bungeed off in *Goldeneye!*'), or on gastronomic tours of Europe ('Anthony Bourdain said this place does the best frikadeller in Copenhagen'). Holidays are planned with precision, with highly detailed itineraries written six months in advance of any trip. We will compile spreadsheets and PowerPoints full of detailed maps, up-to-date menus and museum opening times. Every art gallery, brunch spot and photo op is accounted for and, where possible, semi-committed to memory. If our partners or children attempt to deviate from the itinerary in any way, there's a real risk that the holiday will be ruined, especially if it means we will be seen in public holding a map or guidebook, revealing that we don't actually know our holiday destination like a native after all. Nothing could be more humiliating than for the local 'Bobo Papas' (the International Hipster Dads we encounter abroad) to be unimpressed.

Middle (age) of the road:

the Ultra-Modern Dad behind the wheel

Not that all holidays have to take place outside
the UK. If we're staycationing, Hipster Dads will be
leading tours of the Peak District or Northumbrian
coast in our vintage campervans, despite the fact
that they are famously prone to breakdowns and
give our youngest children explosive carsickness.
That's simply the price you pay for embracing the
ups and downs of Van Life, which all UMDs have
either already done, are planning to do or are
worrying we've missed our moment, now that our
kids are as tall as us and will no longer fit in
a pop-up roof compartment.

But those are the sort of practical considerations
that should never get in the way of owning a
campervan. Can you even call yourself a Hipster
Dad, if you don't have one in the driveway or

the local repair shop? It matters not that we've been renovating ours for fifteen years and that it's barely roadworthy, or that it had done 150,000 miles before we bought it and has done 500 since. We post at least five photos of it on social media each week (it has its own account and 'catchy' name: Sharon Van Etten, Lee Van Cleef, Dita Van Teese, etc.) and that's what matters.

The same criteria applies to any UMD-appropriate vehicle: will it look good on the 'gram? For us, in any list of car-buying must-haves, sensible things like boot space and baby-seat compatibility come a distant second to bonnet badges and boomboxes. If it's prone to regular breakdowns, it's probably a Hipster Dad car.

Hipster Dad family cars	vs	Mainstream Dad family cars
Volkswagen Type 2 Camper (score bonus UMD points if it has a 1960s split windscreen)		Nissan Qashqai
BMW 3 series (but only if it's pre-1995)		Dacia Duster
Any MINI (score bonus points if it's a two-door variety and you have three kids)		Ford Focus
Jeep (especially the big ones; the more impractical for the narrow school-run streets the better)		All Volvos and Vauxhalls
Subaru Impreza (ideally one of the rally-style ones with a ridiculous rear spoiler)		Any Tesla (Hipster Dads think Elon Musk is a right tosser)
Converted ice-cream van or London black cab		Anything that could be described as an SUV or MPV

CHAPTER SEVEN

Sport

This sporting midlife

A nerd by nature (we've somehow managed to catalogue our vinyl collection in both alphabetical order *and* by genre), most Hipster Dads were probably fairly rubbish at sport at school. Perhaps our compulsion to be cooler than the other dads on the block stems from the lifelong trauma of being everyone's last pick in PE. We've been fighting that crushing feeling ever since, and now embrace participatory sport with gusto.

As with most of our passions, we're extremely choosy about sports; we are passionate about the ones we like, and bursting with disdain for the ones we don't. We will not compromise those views, and expect our loved ones to share our sporting preferences. We assume our kids will unquestioningly want to join us on the sofa to watch the action with us. We take it for granted that they will support our teams, and – crucially – expect them to be not quite as good as us at the sports we play together.

We're always up for trying the latest under-the-radar activity, especially if it affords us another opportunity to educate our children, boast to other men our age and to invest in bulky, expensive gear – jai alai scoop, teqball table, single-seater kayak – that will soon be gathering dust in the garage and (for some reason) infuriating our partners. We will sometimes try to rally the local dads to share our niche sporting interests, although our attempts to start a local footgolf or Ultimate Frisbee league are doomed.

We will have more success with our kids, on the basis that they don't have a choice in the matter. New sports will be introduced to our children via a series of fun-filled yet highly competitive family outings. Like Brian Glover's sadistic PE teacher in the film *Kes*, we'll adopt the dual role of both star player and head coach, and impart our insights and wisdom with fervour, despite the fact that we first heard of our latest favourite sport just two weeks ago, and are already discussing it with the tactical nous of Pep Guardiola.

Sometimes we'll seek additional professional guidance. In the face of mixed levels of enthusiasm, we will enrol ourselves and our children in beginner sessions in bouldering, padel, parkour, skateboarding, aikido and more. Our kids are secretly delighted when we pick up an inevitable midlife injury. Although they find it curious that the injuries only seem to occur when we're losing.

Hipster Dad sports	vs	Mainstream Dad sports
Non-league football		Premier League football
Mini golf		Golf
Snowboarding		Skiing
Surfing		Swimming
Pickleball		Squash
Women's rugby		Men's rugby
Darts		Snooker
Formula E		F1
Japanese baseball		Test cricket

Cycle of life: Hipster Dads on two wheels

If there's a sport that sums up what the Ultra-Modern Dad is all about, and embodies our twin obsessions (ridiculously flashy kit and an almost-psychotic competitiveness), it's cycling.

To most people it might look like a few hunks of welded tubing with a couple of wheels attached, but the humble bicycle is to the Hipster Dad a combination of priceless artwork and favourite sex toy: a precious artefact to be revered, studied, admired – and then ridden furiously until we're physically spent.

As a general observation, the UMD will own at least three bikes, from NASA-grade, carbon-fibre road bikes to indestructible off-road mountain bikes (we insist on calling them MTBs), which we will proudly show off to other members of our local cycling club (the Hipster Dad equivalent of Marlon Brando's biker gang).

We may have a favourite bike – the bikes may even have names – but we will geek out over them all equally: pimping, preening, stroking and admiring them with a level of attention and a look of pure pride our middle child can only dream of. They are kept in tip-top Concours condition, should they be required for a 100-mile sportive at a moment's notice, even though they're mostly used for ten-minute trips to the local fishmonger's.

Our bike collections may extend to a couple of vintage curios; perhaps a 1980s Raleigh Grifter or Diamondback BMX, which we will wheel out for special occasions only, such as school parents' evenings. We absolutely Will Not Ever own a fold-up Brompton, which represents the pinnacle of substance over style – everything that is wrong with the modern world, in our eyes.

We may also have a day-to-day bike (still pretty flash by most people's standards), one that we're reluctantly prepared to attach a toddler's tagalong trailer to, even though it feels like a brutal act of aesthetic sacrifice akin to putting a crash helmet on the Mona Lisa. We'd rather be seen in public on a bike purposely designed for the act of carrying multiple passengers. We're not against the idea of a vintage tandem, but we're more likely to be spotted desperately attempting to steer one of those elongated European cargo bikes (we like to remind people that 'it's called a *bakfiets*, actually') with the turning circle of an eight-berth narrowboat. There are usually at least two silently sobbing toddlers in the front crate and our partners say that owning it is an act of filicide waiting to happen.

We relish and dread in equal measure the beautiful/painful day when it will be time to teach our kids how to ride a bike by themselves.

On the one hand it means welcoming another enthusiastic soul to the cycling fraternity, and someone to share our campervan's bike rack with. But, on the other, it's the start of a frustrating, several-year spell during which the little guys won't be able to keep up with our blistering Mark Cavendish-esque pace. It will be like cycling with a stag party after a twelve-pint bender. But that's better than when they leave us eating their dust, of course (and that day is coming soon, too).

UMD FC: Hipster Dads on the terraces

The Ultra-Modern Dad's favourite sport? What else could it possibly be apart from football? We are truly die-hard fans, obsessing over results, tactics and transfer gossip. We listen to all the latest football podcasts and subscribe to multiple soccer-themed newsletters and apps. God, we love football, which our partners find slightly odd because, as they enjoy pointing out in public, we only liked golf and cricket when they met us.

Unsurprisingly, we're pretty picky about the football we like, and it needs to fit within the strict parameters of our UMD worldview. We rarely tune in to *Match of the Day*, preferring to watch Italy's Serie A via a dodgy VPN. We loudly profess our preference for the German Bundesliga over the Premier League ('the atmosphere is just far more authentic, and the Ultras are actually very friendly') and we've half-jokingly vowed to disinherit our nine-year-old for covering his bedroom wall with Arsenal posters. We have a collection of old-school replica shirts and other assorted merch, from pin badges to tote bags to socks, almost entirely sourced online (of course we've never actually *been* to a St Pauli game). Our Kidderminster Harriers snood and Dulwich Hamlet bobble hat are central elements of our weekend winter wardrobe.

We've been dragging our children to watch local non-league games since before they started primary school, and are oblivious to the fact that they consider the Eastern Counties League to be one of the seven circles of Hell. Standing behind the goal in a February hailstorm feels, to them, like a bizarre and wholly unnecessary form of parental torture, or perhaps punishment for a crime committed in a past life. After two years, they still can't name a single player. By the time they start secondary school, they've given up on football completely – a moment made more heartbreaking when they say: 'I don't know why you're so annoyed, Dad. Grandad says you didn't like football at all until you were thirty-five.'

The Ultra-Modern Dad and exercise

It's hard to believe, judging by the overweight photos of us in our late twenties (a blip!), but the UMD is a man who has embraced the fitness boom – and when we say 'embraced', we mean 'got into it before everyone else'.

We are engaged in a lengthy war of attrition with our Dad Bods – with both sides never quite making significant territorial gains – but we are driven by the firm belief that being a bit lardy is not a cool look, especially when trying to dress like a 27-year-old.

So we put the hours in. We've been a Parkrun veteran since well before the local mums made it uncool, and we jog in a Tough Mudder T-shirt, even though didn't finish after having a whitey under a giant fishing net. We talk a lot about 'moving up to triathlon', but it's taking longer than expected because of our clicky hips and arthritic knees.

We proudly tell other dads that we got really into ice baths during the pandemic and are passionate advocates of the Wim Hof method. We even installed one in the garden – though it's actually just a wheelie bin full of rainwater. We haven't been near it since that time when we spent forty-five minutes trying to clamber out of it, convinced we were having a fatal coronary.

We feel safer at the local gym. We've started taking our teenage kids with us, but are considering quitting because our sons can now pull more weight than us on the lat machine and outpace us on the rower, and unlike us aren't scared of hanging out with gym bros in the free weights section. How have our boys developed biceps twice the size of ours, and so quickly?

It's likely that we will have secretly hired an expensive personal trainer without telling our families, so that we don't get left behind.

The Last Word

Ultra-Modern Grandads:

when Hipster Dads get really old

Research published in 2024 in the journal *Psychology and Aging* found that over the past few decades people's perception of old age has been changing rapidly, and that it's increasingly defined as beginning later and later in life. That's partly because individuals are staying healthier for longer, but – let's be honest – it might also be because Gen X and older Millennials are in fierce denial about the ageing process. We're far more likely than previous generations of midlifers to see ourselves as being *really quite young actually* and cling to our youthful interests and behaviour, even though the haunted, Dorian Gray-esque image in the mirror is telling a very different story.

Which begs the question: is there an upper age limit for being trendy? And the supplementary but even more urgent question: 'How many good years do I have left?' If there ever was a limit, we can be sure it's rising. We can also be certain that a new archetype is fast-emerging: the Ultra-Modern Grandad – retired but relevant, grey but groovy, withered but with-it, downsizing but down-with-the-grandkids. If anyone thought the rise of the Hipster Dad was embarrassing, wait till they start spotting the trendy even-older version. Look out for pensioners on vintage Vespas instead of mobility scooters, proffering children wasabi peas instead of Werther's Originals, wearing dental grillz instead of false teeth and chunky DJ headphones instead of hearing aids. Those men will live by the Abe Lincoln motto: it's not the years in your life that count. It's the life in your years.

Expect Gen Z to be very, very confused.

Still Got It?

So there you have us, the Ultra-Modern Dads. The middle-aged men of the moment, in all our trendy, foody, sporty, stylish glory.

And, at the end of the day, what is the rest of the world to make of us? Will our kids and partners ever really understand? Do they look upon us with fondness or as a figure of fun? Do we command their respect, or sympathy? Are our efforts to be cooler than our children ultimately doomed? Are we going through the manopause and having a low-level midlife menty b and, if so, should everyone cut us some slack? Do we need saving from ourselves? Questions, questions.

It would be easy to dismiss us as just another middle-aged cliché, but hopefully people will learn that there's much more to us than that.

For decades, dads have been the butt of pop-culture jokes, often unfairly. Almost all sitcom dads are weak, small-minded fools. The entire TV advertising industry has been built on the idea that all dads are essentially clueless, clumsy buffoons. Hipster Dads may be many things, but we're not those things.

At worst, our obsessions are essentially harmless. But, more than that, they are the glaringly obvious tells of a person who genuinely *cares* about things, possibly a little too much – a man with high standards who won't settle for mediocrity. Doesn't the world need more people like that?

What's more (world's-tiniest-violin alert), being a middle-aged man in the modern world isn't always a picnic. Nobody wants to be getting fatter and balder, or to feel that their best days are behind them and that half the population thinks they're hopelessly out of touch. Grumpiness sets in for a reason. But while midlife can be hard, there is an upside: being a father is a blessing, whether it's to babies, toddlers, tweens or teens – and every Ultra-Modern Dad knows this, intuitively. In answer to the perennial question, why does the UMD do all these cringey, embarrassing things, there's one overriding answer. Because we think our kids are amazing and we want them to think we're amazing, too. We may be an infuriating try-hard at times, but our hearts are definitely in the right place. Give us the love we deserve, people. Just don't touch our Chemical Brothers LPs without asking us first.